1   Mr William Saxby, the Dartford Postman, photographed in his donkey cart in 1870

2 (*overleaf*)   Near the Fish Market, Folkestone, in 1912. On the left is the Fish Auction Shed and on the right The Net House and the Tanlade, where the nets were tanned; this was provided by the William Harvey Charity for the fishermen of the town

Victorian and Edwardian

KENT

from old photographs

Introduction and commentaries by

MARCUS CROUCH

and

WYN BERGESS

PORTMAN BOOKS
LONDON

This edition published 1987 by
Portman Books an imprint of
B. T. Batsford Ltd
4 Fitzhardinge Street, London W1H 0AH

Printed and bound in Great Britain by
Anchor Brendon Ltd, Tiptree, Essex

First published 1974
Text © Marcus Crouch and Wyn Bergess 1974

ISBN 0 7134 2886 4

CONTENTS

ACKNOWLEDGMENTS

For permission to reproduce photographs from their collections the Author and Publishers would like to thank the following:

Gordon Anckorn (Pls 54, 132); Mrs W. F. Bergess (Pl. 58); Bromley Public Library (Pls 12, 13, 71, 77, 134, 149, 153, 157); Canterbury Public Library (Pls 3, 17, 20, 55, 160, 164); E. Course (Pl. 115); Chatham Public Library (Pls 29, 148); Dartford Public Library (Pls 1, 6, 63, 73, 85, 98, 102, 136, 137, 140); Dover Public Library (Pls 30, 31, 32, 99, 107, 110, 116, 158, 168); Eastgate House Museum (Pls 27, 28, 64, 92, 155); Folkstone Public Library (Pls 75, 103, 108, 111, 133, 135); Greater London Council (Pl 67); Kent County Library (Pls 4, 5, 15, 16, 44, 76, 97, 100, 114, 127, 161); Lewisham Public Library (Pls 7, 8, 9, 70); London Transport Executive (Pl. 10); Maidstone County Library (Pls 2, 21, 24, 33, 37, 45, 47, 52, 53, 56, 57, 106, 109, 166); Mansell Collection (Pls 25, 129, 150, 151); Margate Public Library (Pls 120, 123, 126, 138); Marylebone Cricket Club (Pl. 131); Museum of British Transport (Pls 94, 96); Museum of English Rural Life, Reading University (Pls 81, 82); National Maritime Museum (Pls 14, 86, 87, 130); National Monuments Record (Pls 61, 62, 90); Radio Times Hulton Picture Library (Pl. 152); Ramsgate Public Library (Pls 35, 74, 104); Royal Library, Windsor Castle (Pls 34, 59, 142–147); Sevenoaks Public Library (Pl. 46); Stone Collection, Birmingham Public Library (Pls 18, 19, 65, 68, 69); Tonbridge Historical Society (Pls 48, 60, 89, 93, 159, 162, 167); Tunbridge Wells Public Library (Pls 39–42, 66, 72, 95, 141, 163). Plates 3, 11, 22, 23, 36, 38, 43, 49, 50, 51, 78, 79, 80, 83, 84, 88, 91, 101, 105, 112, 113, 117, 118, 119, 122, 124, 125, 128, 139, 154, 156 are from the Publisher's collection.

Special thanks are due to Major R. St G. Bartelot, Curator of the Royal Artillery Regimental Museum, Woolwich and Lt. Col. J. E. South, Librarian of the Royal Military School of Engineering, Chatham.

3   Beating the Bounds of the Parish of St Stephen, Canterbury, September 1903. The Bounds are beaten as an official survey of the Parish boundary line and any encroachments noted or removed. The ceremony takes place at varying intervals of from one to three years and many customs are attached to the event – small boys used to be beaten as an aid to memory at certain points! Now the boundary itself is beaten with willow wands instead, as can be seen in the photograph

INTRODUCTION

Thanks to the retention of ancient privileges, notably a curious custom of land tenure, Kent escaped to some extent the rigours of feudalism, and retained into the nineteenth century an unusual degree of social independence. In this it was helped by a geographical position which discouraged stagnation. London exerted an ever-increasing pressure on the north-western borders, and well-to-do Londoners, fleeing from the urban wrath to come, penetrated deeper into the hinterland in their quest of rustic peace coupled with easy access to the metropolis. With so fluid a population, and with comparative freedom from the industrialisation which, in the north, was producing a new form of serfdom, Kent avoided domination by aristocratic or factory masters.

The great families were still there nevertheless. West Kent especially had become a favoured home of the new aristocracy in Tudor times. There were Sackvilles at Knole. To be more correct there were Sackville-Wests, for the

Dukedom of Dorset had become extinguished with the death, in a hunting accident, of the boy duke who had been Byron's fag and friend at Harrow, and Knole passed through the female line to the lesser glories of a barony. The Sidneys were still their neighbours at Penshurst, and the Darnleys occupied Cobham. Earl Stanhope, Lord Lieutenant in 1890, was of a younger family and occupied a symbolically modern (1630 vintage) house at Chevening. Earl Amherst, descended from the hero of the conquest of Canada, lived at Montreal outside Sevenoaks. Lord Radnor, whose family seat was in Wiltshire, was making perhaps a more positive contribution to Kentish life; he was busy turning his Folkestone estates into the premier watering-place in Kent, if not in England. All these noble lords were but parvenus to Colonel Sir Howland Roberts, a mere baronet but one whose ancestors had settled near Goudhurst in 1103 and whose cousin still occupied the moated manor-house of Glassenbury.

In a remarkable autobiographical sketch – *A Boy in Kent* – C. Henry Warren recalled the working of feudalism in a Kentish village at the end of the old century. There was a 'Jacob's Ladder' of social distinction in church; 'the higher up we were, the nearer we were to God'. Last to arrive for morning service and nearest to the altar was Her Ladyship and 'not until she was seated . . . did the vicar dare to come out of the vestry'. Warren's 'Fladmere' was Mereworth and it is to be noted that Her

Ladyship came from the Palladian 'castle' rather than from the less splendid Court. The castle folk played no considerable part in village affairs; Her Ladyship was reverenced not so much for any practical power which she might wield but because she chose to live among the villagers. The feudalism of Fladmere was largely voluntary.

It was the influence, direct and indirect, of London which led to a phenomenal increase in population during the nineteenth century. The population doubled between 1801 and 1871 and had more than quadrupled by the end of the century (although this did not show in official figures because a large and profitable area had been 'hived off' for the benefit of the new London County Council in 1888). Predictably, the increase was greatest on the London fringe and in fashionable residential areas like Folkestone, in Chatham and Gillingham where the growing naval dockyard created a demand for labour, and in the expanding port of Dover. In the country the population remained static or declined. Waltham, a large (in acreage) parish near Canterbury, had 383 inhabitants in 1801. These had grown to 576 by 1851, but the depression in agriculture had its effect and by 1901 the population was down to 360. In Wormshill, with 1476 acres, the population figure in 1801 was 157, 209 in 1851 and 169 in 1901; by 1911 it had fallen to 138. Compare with this the growth of newly industrialised villages in the cement belt of the Medway, where Burham had 144 inhabitants in 1801 and 1725 in 1901, and Snodland 312 in 1801, 3133 in 1901, and this growth continued into the twentieth century. There was a comparable growth in suburban villages like Eltham (1627 in 1801, 7218 in 1901, 13,450 in 1911) and Orpington (693 in 1801, 4259 in 1901, 5036 in 1911).

Population accurately reflected the changes in habits and occupations. Kent shared in the national depression of agriculture in the second half of the nineteenth century, caused by massive imports of food from Europe and America. In a county which was still, in 1901, predominantly rural in acreage, only 8% of the employed population were occupied in agriculture, compared with over 13% in domestic service. The latter formed by far the largest single class in the community, more than twice as many as those working in the building industry (the third largest group) and more than three times as many of those engaged in engineering. In farming, nevertheless, Kent was better equipped than most English counties to survive the onslaught of foreign competition because of the versatility of the industry. Arable was on the whole poor, except in Thanet, wheat being grown mainly for straw. Market gardening and soft fruit prospered towards London, where strawberries were grown on a large scale and taken to the London markets by train. The great staples of Kentish farmers were, however, hops, fruit and sheep. Hops reached their zenith in 1878; they declined thereafter but still made up the county's principal crop, and a migrant labour-force swelled the native population by something between 45,000 and 65,000 during the weeks of hop-picking. Under the pressure of competition Kentish hop-growers improved their methods, abandoning the traditional 'hills' in which a few bines were trained up a central pole in favour of wires and strings fixed to a permanent layout of poles in rows. Hops were to be found in every part of Kent, although gardens were not numerous in the high Weald and on Romney Marsh. Fruit farming was more local, the best areas lying in the North Kent belt between the Medway Estuary and Canterbury, a traditional home of cherries and apples. By the end of the nineteenth century some of the practices of fruit culture which one thinks of as modern had been adopted – intensive feeding, grading, packing, storing, as well as selling on the tree, and much fruit was being sold to jam factories at Swanley and Sittingbourne. To the familiar Kentish sights of hop gardens and orchards in blossom and fruit must be added another as characteristic of the county – the green levels of Romney Marsh displayed their thousands of hardy, heavy-fleeced sheep, and flocks as fine could be found on Sheppey. Their wool no longer fed a local cloth industry, but Kentish mutton was a favourite item on the menus of innumerable seaside hotels and boarding-houses.

Although the drift to the towns jeopardised the labour supply to farmers, the industry was on a business footing at the end of the century and farmers sent their sons for expert technical training at the South Eastern Agricultural College at Wye. Other traditional occupations were less healthy. In the home of Kentish broadcloth less than 20 people were engaged in weaving. Paper-making, which had been a Kentish industry from its first importation into England, was doing well. Paper needs a supply of the right kind of water and the original mills consequently stood on streams like the Darent, the Len, the Loose and the Shote in West Kent and on the Great Stour in the East. Turkey Mill on the Len had been started by James Whatman in the eighteenth century and was still a going concern, as was the equally old mill at Tovil on the Loose. These establishments, and later mills at Basted and Roughway on the Shote and at Chartham on the Stour, were engaged in the production of quality papers. By the late nineteenth century the heavy battalions had moved in, and huge mills were built at Dartford (making newsprint for the *Daily Telegraph*) and at Northfleet and Kemsley. Edward Lloyd at Kemsley was the first to use esparto grass on a large scale, and this was later superseded by wood-pulp, imported in enormous quantities and requiring deep-water wharves on the Thames and the Medway.

The Industrial Revolution came late to Kent. (In one sense it came very early, for the Weald was the Black Country of England in the great days of iron in the sixteenth century.) Large-scale industrial development did not come, except to some Thames-side areas, until modern planning procedures were able to soften its impact a little. In the Victorian age the biggest single industry, although very restricted in area, was cement. There were seemingly inexhaustible supplies of chalk within easy reach of water, and in the course of the century the face of the county was changed beyond repair. The huge pits dug between Stone and Gravesend (in one of which were discovered the fragmentary remains of Swanscombe Man) remain as a perpetual embarrassment to the authorities and as a monument to the traditional improvidence of industry. In 1901, 1100 cement workers were employed in Northfleet alone, and there were other large workings along the tidal Medway around Burham. Because of these activities the old village of Burham became depopulated and a large new village grew up on the flank of the chalk downs, with a large – and not very handsome – church added to it in 1881.

Another major Kentish industry had its seeds in the Victorian age, although big profits came only at the end of the Edwardian. The existence of a Kentish coalfield had long been known theoretically, but the actual discovery was a by-product of the Channel Tunnel. Work had already been started at the English end of the Tunnel when the government took fright and brought it to a stop in 1882. The workings at Shakespeare's Cliff provided a convenient base for experimental borings which in time proved that coal was there in viable quantities but always at a very great depth. By 1900 several pits were working in East Kent, but the real break-through came with the opening of the Snowdown Colliery in 1908 and another four years passed before this reached its most profitable levels.

Meanwhile the railway age had come to Kent. It had in fact come prematurely, for the Whitstable–Canter-bury line was opened in 1830, before the Rainhill Trials formally ushered in the new age. The Whitstable–Canter-bury was technically ineffective; its one locomotive could not manage the gradients and was too tall for the tunnel, and horses and gravity had to be called into service. The South-Eastern Railway was however quickly a commercial success. The main line from Redhill to Ashford, including the phenomenally straight track between Paddock Wood and Ashford, was constructed in 1842, and extensions to Dover and Margate via Canterbury followed quickly. The

4   The Sands in the Main Bay, Broadstairs, *c.* 1910. Bleak House, where Charles Dickens stayed for a number of years between 1850–59 stands on the cliff on the right. It was castellated in 1902.
   The landward end of the Pier is on the extreme right; it was almost rebuilt after a severe gale damaged the old 'Banjo Jetty' in 1897

railway transformed the little market town of Ashford which doubled its population in the first half-century and was six times larger by 1901. In 1849 the South-Eastern established its railway works here, in which at least a tenth of the inhabitants were employed. The short cut from London to Tonbridge and so on to Dover came much later. By that time a rival company had opened up the North-Kent coast with the London Chatham and Dover Railway, stimulating the growth of the Medway towns and giving a great boost to the holiday trade of the old port of Whitstable and the brand-new township of Herne Bay. These communications accelerated the flow not only of people from London to holidays in Kent but of a reverse process, the beginnings of that apparently twentieth-century phenomenon, commuterdom.

It was the commuter more than the industrialist who transformed the face of Kent. Industry was highly localised, and the Edwardian traveller might cross the county without being much aware of it. He would certainly notice the new houses. The Mr Pooters of the new age lived near their work in terrace houses of the inner suburbs; their masters ringed the city with fantastic mansions, gabled, turretted, mullioned with a splendid disregard of the architectural conventions. William Morris and his friend Philip Webb may have achieved a poem, if a minor one, in warm brick and tile at Bexley; their contemporaries and successors did not mind doggerel if it were flamboyant enough. They wanted something to show for their money, and a journey even today around Bickley and Petts Wood reveals how well they succeeded. The tide of extravagance flowed deep into Kent, super-commuters taking advantage of the railways to put their mock Gothic, baronial and castellated, in favoured parts of Margate and Hythe. A comparable spirit of adventure, fostered by wealth and not too heavily fettered by good taste, led to the erection of many new churches, especially in the mushroom towns which had outgrown their medieval parishes, and, more regrettably, sometimes replacing or overwhelming older foundations in the country. Of the latter Shipbourne is a pretty good essay in Early English, if no compensation for the loss of one of the rare Georgian village churches in Kent and that one by Gibbs. At Speldhurst the old church was lost by lightning and there is now an agreeable replacement of the 1880s with a gallery of late Victorian glass. One could continue at length, but space allows only for a mention of the highlight of Victorian Kent in Pugin's masterpiece of St Augustine's, Ramsgate, where Gothic is revealed not as an academic exercise but as a new discovery.

The charms – freedom from industry, convenience to the City and the Continent, rural pleasures combined with domestic comfort – which attracted the commuter to Kent appealed also to many men of distinction in the worlds

5   Middle-class Kent.
  Children at play in Ashley Avenue, Folkestone, *c.* 1905; a narrow passage leads to the Brickyard between the houses in the background and Tile Kiln Lane is to the right

of literature, art and learning. Edward Hussey put into practice his theories of the picturesque at Scotney. Alfred Austin, Poet Laureate in the direct line from Nahum Tate and Pye, played the country squire at Swinford Old Manor. Ellen Terry created for herself a new rôle, that of benevolent tyrant, in the tiny community of Smallhythe. Darwin found at Downe the peace and content-

ment in which to plan a scientific revolution. Tennyson and Thackeray lived briefly in the county, and George Eliot joined the hordes who flocked to enjoy the delights of – in Mr Pooter's words – 'Good Old Broadstairs'. The literary world was dominated by the reputation of Dickens, who, in every respect but birth, was a Man of Kent.

Despite the paper and cement mills,

the suburban sprawl, the incursion of many who regarded the county as a dormitory rather than a rooted home, the essential Kent of Canterbury and Tenterden, hops and apples, pilgrims and cricketers, survived and with it a strangely revived sense of pride and identification with the past. The Association of Men of Kent and Kentish Men, among the earliest and the most vigorous of county associations, focused attention on events and traditions which, even if transformed out of all recognition by nostalgia, were of inestimable value in strengthening Kent to resist the pressures of the new age.

MARCUS CROUCH

METROPOLITAN KENT

6 Floods in Hythe Street, Dartford, 1895. Parts of the market stalls are used as 'bridges' to the shop doors. In the foreground, High Street joins Hythe Street, and, in 1895, George Vinter's Fish and Poultry Shop was No. 4 High Street and Tailor Priessnitz Jones was next door at No. 2. John Upson and Co., Bootmakers, occupied Nos. 15 and 25 High Street, but appear to have temporary premises after a fire

7 The Clock Tower was erected in Lewisham High Street to commemorate the Diamond Jubilee of Queen Victoria in 1897. On the right is Robert Lydall's stationery shop at 71A High Street and, next door, George Strand occupies Nos. 65–69 High Street with his fancy drapery, silk mercery and china and glass warehouse. A fully laden horse-drawn 'bus is passing the shop

8 Horse buses make their leisurely way along Lee Road, Lee Green, *c.* 1895. The 'Old Tigers' Head' stands on the left hand corner and the 'New Tigers' Head', built in 1887, is on the right

9 Blackheath Village, *c.* 1905. The horse-drawn traffic climbs up steep Lee Road and the graceful spire of All Saints' Church soars in the background

10 Three cars of the L.C.C. Tramways converging at New Cross Gate, *c.* 1912. They were open-topped double-deckers with reversed stairs. The 'White Hart' Hotel was built *c.* 1895 and still survives

11 Part of the Market in Beresford Square, Woolwich, *c.* 1880. Workers are leaving the Royal Arsenal, enlarged by the Dockyard buildings, closed in 1869. A white horse-tram of the London–Greenwich route stands outside.

Note the elegant wrought-iron urinal of 1884, in the true 'Clochemerle' tradition

12 'The Bell' Hotel, High Street, Bromley, *c.* 1895. A Posting House, by Appointment to Queen Victoria, and a meeting place for influential townsmen, it was demolished in 1897. The two stone balls above the shop front beyond the Hotel once surmounted the gate piers of the lodges (on this site) of Crete House, the 'finest mansion in Bromley'

13 The 'Rising Sun', High Street, Bromley in 1856. It was the Headquarters of the Society of Bromley Youths (bellringers). The landlord, George Porter, was a Lincolnshire man and he supplied the bellringers with liquid refreshment after ceremonies calling for bells. The Police House was entirely rebuilt in 1899. Next door was Samuel Porter's drapery business at 36/37 High Street. The Police station moved to this position in 1841 and the 'Rose and Crown' beyond faced into the Market Place

14 A meeting of the ways in Gravesend, *c.* 1870.

In the foreground is New Street with the 'Nelson Tap' on the corner of Stone Street. Further down on the right is the 'Lord Nelson' Inn and Posting House with Windmill Street corner beyond it also on the right. Princes Street is on the left, behind the policeman, and the turning into High Street is hidden by the carts. King Street runs beyond into the background, Caddel's Printing Office being No. 1

15 King Street, Gravesend, 1902, with the entrance to High Street on the left. Caddel's Printing Office on the left was founded by John Samuel Caddel, stationer, bookbinder, stamp distributor and publisher of the *Gravesend Journal* until a decade before. Tramcars have made their appearance since the photograph of 1870

TOWNS

16 Mercery Lane, Canterbury, c. 1890, a medieval street which is virtually unchanged today – even to the repair work being carried out on the cathedral

17 Steeplejacks at work on the pinnacles of Bell Harry Tower

18 The Very Revd Henry Wace D.D., photographed in Canterbury Cathedral Precincts in 1906. Dean of Canterbury 1903–1924, he had a distinguished clerical career including service as Hon. Chaplain to Edward VII in 1902

19 Cathedral choristers en route for choir practice in 1906. The Choir School, probably dating from medieval times, was closed in 1972

20 Christ Church Gate in Sun Street, 1890. The face is deeply pitted as the result of damage caused by Commonwealth soldiers. Note the street traders

21 The City Wall, Canterbury in 1910, a promenade then, as now, above the Dane John Gardens

MAIDSTONE

22 Medway Barges moored at the wharves below the new Maidstone Bridge in 1891 (this replaced the old bridge in 1879). The Tower of All Saints Church and the Archbishop's Palace can be seen on the left beyond the Bridge. The warehouses were occupied by millers and corn-merchants

23 The upper part of the High Street, Maidstone, in 1898 with the Town Hall on the right and Queen Victoria's statue in the background

24 The lower end of the High Street, Maidstone in 1891, showing Middle Row and Bank Street on the right

ROCHESTER

25 Rochester Bridge, *c.* 1900. This was the fourth construction, built of iron in 1856–7, when the old brick bridge was demolished. In 1914 the cast-iron arched girders were replaced by straight ones to form the fifth bridge construction. Stones and balustrades from the old bridge were used in building the Esplanade on the opposite bank of the River Medway; Rochester Castle and the Cathedral may be seen in the background. In 1904 the pinnacled cathedral tower was reconstructed to simulate the Norman original

26 The steam ship *City of Rochester* was frozen in the Bridge Reach, River Medway, for 12 days in February 1895

27 The City Auction Rooms, Rochester, taken after 1895 when the numbering of the High Street was changed. The premises stand opposite the General Post Office and were originally built for a Wine Merchant of Chatham. Mr Thomas Peters and Mr Thomas Long stand outside

28 The Old Parr's Head and Parr's Head Lane, Rochester, *c.* 1880. Until 1860, the Old Parr's Head was the 'Club' for better class citizens; it was demolished in 1890 to make way for the S.E. Railway extension. The stone head may be seen in Rochester Museum

29 The High Street, Chatham, *c.* 1900. Thomas Fowle and Sons, 250 High Street, were 'popular' undertakers of the time and specimens of their monumental masonry may be seen, signed, throughout the Medway villages

30 Woolcomber Street, Dover, in 1894, before it was widened; it was so named because the houses were occupied by Woolcombers in the eighteenth century. On the right are the turnings for Trevanion and Wool-comber Lanes, with Broad's Confectionery Shop on the corner of the latter. The sign directing customers to the livery stables indicates the importance of horse transport in Dover before the arrival of the motor car about two years later

31 The junction of St James Street and St James Lane, Dover, *c.* 1890: one of the hazards of the town when the road formed part of the Dover to Deal and Thanet Stage Coach Route. On the right is Jimmy Sedgewick's furniture store with the slatted wooden front of the old Town Mill beyond. The shop on the corner was Dover's oldest pet shop and one of the oldest domestic buildings to survive into the twentieth century. With all the buildings on the left, is has now disappeared

32 Ashen Tree Lane, off Castle Hill, Dover, in 1851. The open country came close to the town centre at this date. The notice reads: 'Milk and Cream sold here by Widow Baker, daughter of the late Widow Clara'

DEAL

33 Beach Street, Deal, at the northern end of the town, in 1906. Boats were launched into the open sea, there being no harbour. Before the lifeboat was built, 'galley punts' were launched for rescue operations

RAMSGATE

34 Harbour Street, Ramsgate, *c.* 1856, looking towards the Royal Hotel. The Albion Hotel was bought by the National Provincial Bank in 1895 and became an extension for the Bank

35 The Harbour at Ramsgate, *c.* 1890, with the Albion Hotel on the left and the clock tower on the Harbour Buildings visible behind the masts of the moored ships at the Town Quay

FOLKESTONE

36 The Eastern end of the Leas, Folkestone, *c.* 1895. On the left, Albion Villas, said to have been built from left-over material from the Railway Viaduct; on the right 'Priory Gardens', with the old Vicarage beyond. Bath chairs and their attendants were for hire to the frail and the elderly

37 The Victoria, or Pleasure Pier, Folkestone, seen here in 1901. It was opened on 21 July 1888. The beginning of the end for this elegant promenade came in 1940, when a section was removed as an anti-invasion precaution. In 1948 the Pavilion at the end of the Pier burnt down and the remains of the Pier was finally removed in 1954–55. Keith Prowse owned it at one period and some of the first Beauty Shows were held on it. On the Leas, above, the houses on the right were the first to be built. Opposite the Camera Obscura is the Leas Lift, constructed in 1885 and still in use

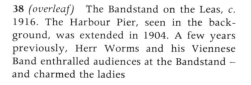

38 *(overleaf)* The Bandstand on the Leas, *c.* 1916. The Harbour Pier, seen in the background, was extended in 1904. A few years previously, Herr Worms and his Viennese Band enthralled audiences at the Bandstand – and charmed the ladies

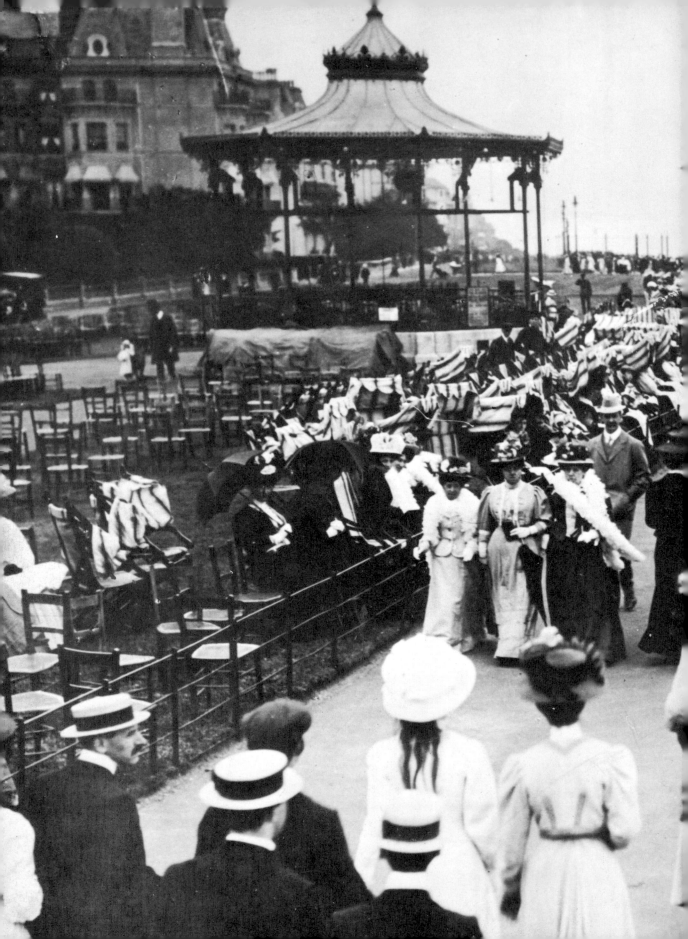

TUNBRIDGE WELLS

39 Chapel Place, Tunbridge Wells, *c.* 1860, with the Church of King Charles the Martyr in the background. Note the elegant wrought-iron lamp bracket on the right

40 The Sweeper in the Pantiles, Tunbridge Wells, *c.* 1880. The Pantiles was built on the site of a Chalybeate Spring discovered by the third Baron North in 1606. The walk was constructed in 1638

41 The Pantiles, Tunbridge Wells, in 1885, then as now a popular promenade. A German Band is playing and behind stands the Corn Exchange, originally the Assembly Rooms and Theatre

42 The South Eastern Station, now the Central Station, Tunbridge Wells, *c.* 1905, with Mount Pleasant ascending beyond it

ASHFORD

43   High Street, Ashford, in 1901, with the Castle Hotel in the background

44   Elwick Road, Ashford, *c.* 1910. Sheep on their way to the Cattle Market (built in 1856) surround the 'Saracen's Head' Hotel conveyance. The Hotel was a posting house and stood on the corner of High Street and North Street, the site now occupied by Sainsbury's Supermarket. It was originally the manorial residence of Essetesford. The pillared building was the Elwick Iron Works of Mr Frederick Clark

SEVENOAKS

45 The London Road, Sevenoaks, *c.* 1895. The rear entrance of the 'Chequers Inn' can be seen on the right; the front of the Inn faces the Cattle Market. The houses in the right background are now shops and a cinema now replaces the large house on the left

46 The Sevenoaks Coffee Tavern divides the London Road (left) from the High Street (right), *c.* 1900. At this time it was owned by Thomas Foster. The Market Place may be seen on the left of the High Street, in front of the Bank. The Tavern, much altered, is now occupied by the Midland Bank

47 The High Street, Sevenoaks, *c.* 1900, with the open space of the Market Place before the Bank

TONBRIDGE

48 Floods in Tonbridge High Street, *c.* 1880, almost an annual event then as now. Mr Charles Wakeford, bootmaker, surveys the scene from a chair in his doorway. William Gale established his bootmaking business before he was 21, in 1875, and it continues to this day under Nelson Gale. Between 1893 and 1905, the buildings on the opposite side of the street were cleared for street widening

49 London Road, Southborough, in 1900. It still presents much the same appearance, but the town merges with Tunbridge Wells now

FAVERSHAM

50 West Street, Faversham, in 1891. In the right foreground is the saddlery and harness maker, Robert Wright's shop on the corner of the Market Place. The town of Faversham is under a preservation order and more than any other town in Kent retains much of its original appearance

TENTERDEN

51 Evidently the season for bowling hoops – the children stand in front of Reuben Barton's hairdressing salon and George Burden's fish and poultry shop in Tenterden High Street, 1907

CRANBROOK

52 Stone Street, Cranbrook, in 1901 – Messrs T. S. Stokes and Sons' Emporium on the left of the Street was a substantial drapery, millinery and dressmaking establishment, and, from the signs on the right, the motor car had evidently arrived if it is not here in evidence. Union Mill, seen in the background, is a fine specimen of a Kentish Smock Mill. It was built in 1814 for Henry Dobell by Millwright Humphry, who lived in Cranbrook and who built other mills in Kent

VILLAGES

53 The centre of Ightham Village in 1901 with three of the many types of horse-drawn vehicles in use at the time. 'The Railway Bell' was only licensed to sell beer, but the 'George and Dragon' and 'The Chequers Inn' both advertised 'good accommodation for cyclists' amongst other hotel facilities. Cycling was then very much in vogue

54 The High Street, Westerham, *c.* 1895, with wicket cattle pens and farm carts outside the 'George and Dragon'. In 1895 the landlord was Robert Jones but the sign reads 'John Jones'. A saddler advertises on the inn-sign

55 The 'Rose and Crown', High Street, Elham, a photograph taken on 16 September 1904. Mrs Sarah Wilson kept the family and commercial hotel with 'good stalling and horses and traps for hire'. Elham was an ancient town and a large parish at this time

56 Typical Kentish cottages in the village of Great Chart in 1908. The village lay under the influence of Godinton, a great house whose park came to the end of the High Street, and the school, the almshouses and many cottages reflected the interest of the family

57 The Church of St Mary and part of the town of Goudhurst is built on a ridge. The photograph shows the steep approach to the Church in 1901

58 The Stables of 'The Homestead', Wouldham, *c.* 1910. The Norris family became carriers and makers of horse-drawn vehicles of all kinds during the mid-nineteenth century. The family and the business still thrive – but coaches and vans have succeeded the hansoms, carts and elegant traps.

From left to right: Jessie Norris, L/Seaman Arthur P. Timothy, R.N. soon to become a Chief Petty Officer, Henry Norris (present occupier of the Homestead), Bertie Norris (on horse), Mr Ernest Norris, Percy Norris, Mrs Sarah Norris and Ernest Norris

NOBILITY AND GENTRY

59 A house party at tea in the garden at Knole, Sevenoaks, photographed on 26 August 1899.
   Victoria Mary, Duchess of York, is seated second from the right with her hand resting on the tea table; Prince Alexander of Teck stands third from the right with Mr Frank Dugdale next to him (wearing the 'boater'). Lady Eva Dugdale is seated on the extreme right

60 Croquet on the vicarage lawn, Tonbridge, *c.* 1865. The tower of the Parish Church of SS Peter and Paul can be seen behind the trees. A new vicarage replaced this charming house in 1960, when it was demolished. Vicar on seat – up to 1864 – Sir Charles Hardinge. *Post* 1864 – Revd John T. Manley.

61–62 Beechmont, near Sevenoaks, was built and occupied by the Lambarde family from *c.* 1830. It is thought to have been built on the site of a Hunting Lodge. In the 1870s, when these photographs were taken, the occupier was Molton Lambarde, Esq. The first shows a group at croquet in front of the house, and the second shows Mrs Lambarde and daughter Alice about to take a drive. During World War II the house was a billet for the A.T.S. and was destroyed by a flying bomb

63   The Revd Percy E. Smith, Vicar of Dartford from 1893–1916, outside his charming vicarage before taking a drive. Mrs Smith and the family pet sit ready in the trap, while her household staff and Mr J. H. Shaw, the Verger (extreme left) look on. *c.* 1910

THE POOR

64 Walter Henry Sergent de Brison – 'Gentleman, soldier and Pedlar' – was well known in the streets of
nineteenth-century Chatham carrying his box and basket of wares and calling

Pins, needles, cottons and thread
Boot laces, stay laces, blacking and black-lead

He was born in Co. Cork in 1824, son of a lieutenant in the Royal Munster Light Infantry and he enlisted
in the 38th Regiment of Foot when 18. Stationed in Chatham, he then embarked from Gravesend in 1844 with
a detachment to join Companies of the Regiment in China and later India. After 12 years he was invalided
home and failed to secure a permanent pension. He lived in poverty and solitude until his emaciated body was
found in his two-roomed hovel in a passage leading from New Road to the Mount in December 1893. Typically,
when he was dead, the public subscribed to his assistance – a funeral and a headstone in Chatham Cemetery

65 Distributing the Biddenden Charity from the Old Work House (built by the Parish in 1779) on Easter Sunday 1902. A charity in the name of Siamese Twins Eliza and Mary Chalkhurst, allegedly born in 1100 – probably a misreading of 1600 – it consists of the revenue from 18 acres of land to be spent in 'bread and beer' for the poor of the village. This gift has been made for over 300 years – with the exception of the beer! Until 1682, the charity was given from the Church, then from the Porch until the end of the nineteenth century, when it was transferred to the Old Work House. The gift now takes the form of small cakes with the figures of the twins stamped upon them

66 The General Hospital, Tunbridge Wells – the Waiting Hall for out-Patients in 1904. The Hospital, fronting on the Grosvenor Road, was supported by voluntary subscriptions and practically rebuilt during 1869–70. An annual subscription of half a guinea or donation of 5 guineas entitled the benefactor to have one out-patient on the books – double these amounts entitled the donor to take his position on the Board of Governors!

SCHOOLS

67   The Boys' Drill Class at the Blackheath Elementary School in 1906, then governed by the Old School Board of London

68–69   The Girls and Boys of Biddenden National School in 1902 when there were 180 'mixed' and 75 infants in attendance under the tutelage of Mr and Mrs A. T. Haughton and their staff of two. The school stands opposite Biddenden Church, seen behind the group of boys, and the present school was built about 100 years ago. The foundations, however, have existed since 1522

70 The interior of the last of the private schools in Deptford, which, prior to 1870, existed in Grove Street. The headmaster, Mr Williams, was also a member of the Old Deptford Vestry – and known to his pupils as 'Bunny'. He is presiding over his pupils in this picture

71 The Bromley National School Infants' Class in 1886, with two charming teachers. The National School came into being in 1814, when it absorbed the Old Charity School under Mr and Mrs Campling. The New School was built on 'School Field', east of Bromley College, for 700 children including the Infants from their separate school at Plaistow, founded in 1847. The Combined New National School was opened on 6 July 1855. In May 1888 elections for the first Bromley School Board were held and the National School as such ended. The Head Teacher in 1886 was Miss Elizabeth Churcher

SHOPPING

72 Tolson and Company's splendid array of fish and game at their Fish Market in the Pantiles, Tunbridge Wells, *c.* 1875. This business ceased in 1925 and the premises are now occupied by CECI – Antique Dealers. The area is still known as the Old Fish Market

73 Simon Francis Phillips, his wife and family are watching their shop being photographed in 1900. Mr Phillips was a draper and furniture warehouseman whose premises occupied Nos. 27, 29 and 31 High Street, Dartford, *c.* 1870–1925. The site is now occupied by Woolworth's

74 'Larry', or Lazarus, Hart of 7 and 9 Harbour Street, Ramsgate, sitting outside his shop, c. 1908. He is styled as a china and glass dealer at this time, but pre-1907 was a general dealer – his stock still fits this description

75 Young sharks caught off Folkestone in 1910. Fishermen took them to show the townspeople their strange catch. Postman Young can also be seen, as well as a handsome tabby cat

76 The Tuesday Market in Bromley, with housewives making a critical choice of greengrocery. Arthur Pardon, bird and animal dealer of 24 Market Square, conducted his business between the years 1909 and 1913, the period at which this picture must therefore have been taken

FARMING

77 Rest and refreshment for the harvesters on Springhill Farm, *c.* 1883. The farm was owned by Major Clement Setterthwaite, to whose family memorial windows can be seen in Plaistow Parish Church. The farm was a quarter of a mile north of Burnt Ash Library on the road to Grove Park

78 Aristocratic hop-pickers at Yotes Court Farm, Mereworth, owned by Viscountess Torrington and renowned for 'one of the choicest little growths in the district'. The harvesters of 1895 photographed here were the Hon. Vera Byng, Mr Evelyn S. Seymour and Viscountess Torrington. Mr T. Edwards, her Bailiff, stands on the right with his dog

79 Londoners waiting for the train to take them home after a hop-picking holiday in Kent, *c.* 1906

80 A sunny day and laughing faces: hop pickers at Cranbrook in 1906. Today, the hops are picked by machine. The picture is probably of Cheesman Bros Farm at Goddard's Green

81 *(overleaf)* Fruit pickers at Paxton Farm, Bewley, Ightham, in 1907. Albert, Frederick and Mrs Phoebe Crowson were fruit-growers in the area

82   Stacking at Ripple Farm, Godmersham, 1913

83   A handsome team of shire horses drawing a cart load of hurdles on a Kentish farm, *c.* 1900

84   A team of oxen and driver on a farm near Tenterden, *c.* 1900. They worked at Bulleign Farm, Smallhythe, and were later moved to Morghew at Tenterden. Other teams were in use at Benenden and Cranbrook

INDUSTRY

85 A group of workmen in Messrs John and Edward Hall's Engineering Works, Hythe Street, Dartford, *c.* 1900. They were styled as 'engineers, iron and brass founders, boiler makers and gunpowder machinery manufacturers', and also made the Hallford Lorry 1905–25. The firm was founded in 1785 and continues as a Division of Hall-Thermotank Ltd., making refrigeration machinery

86 John Rennie, marine engineer and George Rennie, mechanical engineer, set up their shipyard at Norman Road, Greenwich in 1821. They made shallow-draft river steamers in 1859 and diesel engines for naval launches in 1865 – the year in which this photograph of workmen cutting lengths of steel was taken. In 1915 the firm left Greenwich, merging with Forrest and Company of Wivenhoe, and the company of Rennie-Forrest continued until 1930.

The Rennie shipyard was bought by the Tilbury Contracting and Dredging Company in 1915 and this name can still be seen on the gates

87 Interested observers see Mr F. North experimenting with a square buoy in Sheerness Dockyard, 1868. The Naval Dockyard provided work for 1,500–2,000 artisans at this time; now it gives commercial harbourage under the Medway Port Authority to deep water shipping

88 Workers in a Kentish brickfield enjoying their bever – a substantial mid-morning snack usually with beer

89 The Waghorns and their workers outside the Forge in Avebury Avenue, Tonbridge, *c*. 1900. William Waghorn and his son, also William, stand on each side of the central bearded workman

90 Although the Channel Tunnel Act was passed in 1875, the tunnel and shaft between Abbot's and Shakespeare Cliff, near Dover, were not begun until the energetic Sir Edward Watkin (Chairman of the S.E. Railway) came to an understanding with the French Company and an S.E.R. Act of 1881 authorised him to take a hand. A tunnel 7 feet in diameter and a shaft 2,026 feet from the Shakespeare Cliff were started in 1881. A boring machine, called the Beaumont Tunneller after its inventor, Col. Frederick Beaumont, was used and in this photograph chalk from the boring machine is falling from a conveyor belt into a Decauville Wagon.

Sir Edward was a fine Public Relations man and held elegant submarine luncheon parties in the tunnel to boost the shares

TRANSPORT

91 The through service by horse tram from the south side of Westminster Bridge to Greenwich began on 29 January 1872, the cars were white and, in 1884, the service interval was 6 minutes and the through fare 3d! The service was the result of the amalgamation of the Pimlico–Peckham and Greenwich with the Metropolitan Street Tramways Company to form the London Tramways Company Ltd – although Parliamentary Assent was not given until 1873. Tramcar No. 338 is standing outside the tobacconist's shop of Mr H. Waugh, 159 Trafalgar Road, Greenwich, *c.* 1883

92 The Turnpike Gate at the corner of North Street, Strood, *c.* 1870. The gate stretched from the south-west corner of the 'Angel' Inn, rebuilt in 1899 and still in business, to the Workmen's Institute opposite. It was abolished on 30 November 1876 when the Bridge Wardens paid the remainder of the debt. The Clothiers Shop was demolished in 1896

93 A railway accident at Tubs Hill Station, Sevenoaks, in 1884. A collision between two engines caused the deaths of four railway men

94 The re-opening of the S.E. Railway between Folkestone and Dover on 9 March 1877 following a landslide on 12 January 1877, when a storm washed away the foot of the cliff and 60,000 cubic yards fell into the cutting at the southern end of Martello Tunnel; the mound was 116 feet deep, burying and killing three men. The single line here was in use from 12 March 1877 and the second line was cleared by 30 May 1877. Sir Edward Watkin, wearing the Cossack Cap, was Chairman of the S.E. Railway 1866–1894 – as well as of 11 other Railway Companies! The Locomotive is a Cudworth 2–4–0 Class – with a stove pipe chimney

95 The South Eastern Station, Tunbridge Wells in 1880. It was opened to passengers in 1846 and is quite recognisable as the present Central Station, retaining some of the original building on the 'up' side. It is situated between two tunnels in a hollow at the foot of Mount Pleasant, truly in the centre of the town. An 'ironclad' engine draws early small four-wheeled carriages

96 The Squire, the Parson and a less exalted person sitting beneath the decorative nameboard of Hope Mill Station, which was opened on 1 October 1892. The station was later renamed Goudhurst. The line is now closed

97 A 4–4–0 Engine made by James Stirling, *c.* 1898, for the S.E. and C. Railway, steaming into Chilham Station. This station was opened on 6 February 1846. Note the Kentish Oast House behind the train

98 An accident with a traction engine in Overy Liberty, Dartford, *c.* 1883. Mr George Ticehurst, butcher, and Mrs Mary Ann Newman, grocer, could not have been very pleased at the damage to their shop fronts

99 The Old Fish Market at Crosswall, Dover, *c.* 1900, where the fishermen's catches were sold by auction. The Crosswall was originally a floating dock formed by a wall built diagonally across the tidal harbour in 1661.
  Dover Corporation's Electric Trams were installed in 1897, providing a cheap and fast means of transport badly needed in the town. The No 10 tram edges its way through the congestion

100 In the elegant Edwardian era, a coaching revival took place, with many a gentleman fancying himself as a 'whip'; one of these was Sir Algernon Aspinall. This coach-and-four stands outside the Grand Hotel, Folkestone, c. 1910. Note the giant telescope standing in the hotel porch

101 *(left)* Two elegant gentlemen pose aboard a carriage made by Panhard and Levassoc, and with a Daimler Engine, at the Exhibition of Horseless Vehicles held at Tunbridge Wells in October 1895. The bearded gentleman is probably the Hon Evelyn Ellis

102 The Dartford to Farningham bus on the Hawley Road between the Papermakers Public House and Shirehall Road in 1907. Fare 6d for the journey! It was the first omnibus made by J. and E. Hall's Engineering Firm, Dartford, with the bodywork – a char-à-banc body on an early Hallford lorry chassis – built by the firm of George Stubbs of Wilmington. The firm was owned by John Carpenter, and his son, Charles is seated by the test driver for Hall's, Walter Dunmall of Farningham. Mr Williamson sits behind him, the bearded gentleman is Mr Say, and the leady seated at the back, Mrs Wakeling

103 A men-only coach outing setting off, *c.* 1905, from The Harbour Hotel, 24 Harbour Street, Folkestone; next door is the more elegant Carter's 'True Briton' Hotel. The London and South Coast Motor Services Ltd (Managing Director J. W. Cann) specialised in excursions to the South Coast during the summer months

SHIPPING

104 The Ramsgate Lifeboat crew, wearing cork 'lifesavers' who went to the help of the *Indian Chief* in 1881.
The Coxwain was Charles Fish and the crew of 11 included Tom Cooper and Dick Goldsmith. The *Indian Chief*
was sailing from Middlesbrough to Yokohama with a crew of 28 and foundered on the Goodwin Sands.
11 were saved after an afternoon and night of endeavour. The R.N.L.I. recognition of this rescue was an
unprecedented number of awards: Charles Fish won a gold medal and silver medals were awarded to the rest
of the crew and also to the Master and six crew of the tug *Vulcan,* who assisted the lifeboat. Charles Fish
won a second gold medal later in a service during which he had helped to rescue 877 lives. He died in 1915
aged 74

105 Fishing fleet at anchor in Ramsgate Harbour, 1901. The arched Royal Parade obscures the chalk cliff face of earlier years

106 Fishing boats and the Quay at Folkestone, *c.* 1908, with the Fish Market on the right

107 A sailing vessel alongside Commercial Quay, Dover, *c.* 1850. The Quay was built in 1834, when the dock was tidal, and timber piling was used

108 Wrecks of the Norwegian Barques *Baron Holburg* and *Agder* lying on Folkestone beach after the great gale of 25 September 1896

109 Passengers embarking on the S.S. *Mary Beatrice* at Folkestone Harbour en route for Boulogne: August 1894

110 Dover Harbour, showing the twin-hulled *Calais–Douvres* steam packet (with black funnels) alongside the Cross-Wall, *c*. 1885. The three smaller vessels of the Samphire Class (336 tons) were the *Wave, Breeze* and *La France* (1864–99) of the L.C. and D. Railway. The large vessel alongside the buildings of Geo. Hammond and Co.'s works is thought to be *The Prince Imperial,* in service until 1899

111 A Norwegian cargo vessel passing the Horn Lighthouse at the entrance to Folkestone Harbour, *c*. 1880. There was a considerable increase in goods traffic by sea during the nineteenth century

112   This bottle-nosed whale was stranded on the Thames mud at Woolwich, 27 November 1899. The brown-sailed Thames barges were a familiar sight on the River

113   A calm voyage on the S.S. *Ella,* an L.S.W.R. vessel built by Aitken and Mansell in 1881, and sold to the Shipping Federation in 1913

114 *(overleaf)*   Baggage arriving for a special train on board a Channel Packet, *c.* 1910

115 The first visit of S.S. *Deutschland* to Dover, 22 July 1904. The *Deutschland* was launched in 1900 in the presence of the Kaiser. It was the largest and finest liner in the world, but was inconsistent as to speed and did not manage to achieve the Blue Riband of the Atlantic Crossing

116 The *Preussen,* a German five-masted schooner of 5,081 tons, was built of steel by Loeisz and Co. in 1902 and was the largest sailing ship in the world. A heavy gale blew in the Channel on 4–5 November 1910 and the *Preussen* collided with the channel steamer *Brighton* between Newhaven and Dieppe; she lost her jib-boom and sprang a leak forward. Anchored off Dungeness, the anchor cables parted and the *Preussen* was taken in tow by tugs. The tow parted off St Margaret's Bay and the ship ran heavily ashore at the foot of the cliffs; she stayed fast on the rocks for some weeks but another gale raged from 4–11 January 1911 and broke her in two – but not a life was lost

SEASIDE

117   Bathing at Folkestone in 1913

118 Newgate Gap, Margate, was not only a hiring place for donkey rides in 1890 but it was also 'the only entrance to Charlotte Pettman's original Sea-Water Baths' where 'the bathing machines were superior to all others and the purity of the seawater was unsurpassed'

119 Ramsgate Harbour and the West Cliff from the Pier, *c.* 1890. 'Jacob's Ladder', a steep flight of steps leading from the Quay to the cliff top, can just be seen on the left. The foundations for the Arches of the Royal Parade, which now obscure the cliff face, were laid in 1893

120 On Margate Beach, *c.* 1860, in the Palm Bay area. The cliff on the right has disappeared from the action of wind, weather and sea

121 Westgate-on-Sea, a rising and fashionable resort in 1907 and about 1½ miles from Margate. The 'Tower House Retreat' was believed to be the only building in the U.K. erected for the treatment of intemperance in ladies and gentlemen and was founded in 1879 by John H. Brown

122 The Bandstand, Margate, stood on the green between the Cliff Edge and road above the Fort Steps. The excavations for the construction of the Winter Gardens, started about 1898, cut into the cliff below and the Bandstand was demolished

123 The hexagonal extension to Margate Jetty was begun in the autumn of 1875 and was opened by the Lord Mayor of London on 1 January 1877. Less than a year later a drifting wreck caused considerable damage. The extension was designed by G. Gordon Page and cost £25,000

124 The Sands, Promenade Pier, built in 1881 and the Station, Ramsgate, *c.* 1900. This was the terminus of the L.C. and D. Railway and was opened in October 1863. It was closed in July 1926 and now Ramsgate Station is situated at the rear of the town

125   The *New Moss Rose* and *The Prince Frederick William* leaving Ramsgate Harbour *c.* 1905 and passing the West Pier and lighthouse. Behind the pleasure boats the famous steam tug *Aid* may be seen. She was built in 1899, a heavily sparred vessel with a fore royal, and one of her tasks was towing the lifeboat rapidly to ships in distress

126   The Iron Landing Pier, or Jetty, photographed in 1856. The first pile was laid in May 1853 and it was opened on 9 April 1855; a dinner for 1,000 people was given there to celebrate the end of the Crimean War on 29 May 1856. It replaced the old wooden structure, Jarvis' Landing Place, which was named for its designer, David Jarvis M.D. Messrs Bird of London designed the new Jetty and the contractor was Samuel Bastow of Hartlepool. The length was 1,240 feet

127 The *Sunbeam* pleasure yacht takes on passengers at Margate Jetty, *c.* 1910 from which it sailed daily at 11 a.m. and 3 p.m. This was also the embarkation point for London by sea and the River Thames

128 The eastern end of the Marine Parade, Dover in 1894. These houses were destroyed in World War II and have been replaced by modern flats. The bathing machines were advertised as 'numerous and clean' and the sea as 'wonderfully clear'. Dover Castle stands 400 feet above the town, with the Roman Pharos next to St Mary's medieval church

129 Paddling at Ramsgate, c. 1895

SPORTS AND PASTIMES

130   A Cricket Team from the Naval Dockyard at Sheerness, 1867

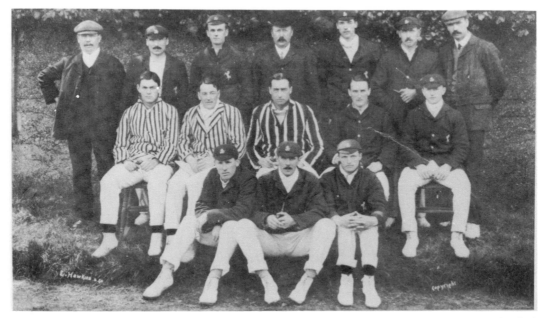

131 Kent County Cricket Team, 1907; a comparatively poor year for the County Team, which finished eighth in the County championship. The bowling was fairly strong but the batting weak. Blythe and Fielder had a splendid bowling season, but Hardinge was the only promising batsman

132 The Vine Cricket Ground in Dartford Road, Sevenoaks, *c.* 1905. It is possibly the oldest cricket ground in England – the first fully reported match, between Kent and Sussex, took place on September 9th 1734 and there was a Bi-Centenary Celebration in 1934. The ground was given to the town 'for ever', *c.* 1778, by John, 3rd Duke of Dorset. The name may have originated from the location of a small vineyard kept to provide wine for the Archbishop of Canterbury by his Bailiff at Sevenoaks – early in the eighteenth century it was known as a 'small plain devoted to Cricketings . . .' The Club buildings on the left included a Hall accommodating 500 people, it was destroyed in World War II. The Constitutional Hall beyond was built in 1890 and is now the headquarters of the Sevenoaks Conservative Association

133   Anyone for Tennis? A group of tennis players pose in a shady corner at Folkestone, *c.* 1900

134   Martin's Hill, Bromley, *c.* 1905. During the mid-nineteenth century the site attracted building prospectors, but eventually Bromley Council bought the land for public recreation for £2,500 in 1878, and other portions of land were purchased and added to it during succeeding years. The Lodge and Drinking Fountain were erected in 1887

135 The first Cycling Club at Folkestone, *c.* 1885. The Stanley 'Royal Salvo' Tricycle appears to be the favourite mount, with only one rider perched on his 'Penny Farthing' at the back of the group

136 Ready for the Maypole Dance at Dartford, *c.* 1896

137 The 'Daren' Bread entry in the Parade held at Dartford in 1911 to celebrate the Coronation of King George V and Queen Mary. The flour was milled by the Keyes brothers at the Daren Mills on Dartford Creek. The business was established at Brent Windmill in 1875 by Leonard Keyes and a move to Colyers Mill coincided with his brother S. K. Keyes joining the firm. In 1891, the Daren Mills on Dartford Creek were purchased and the family business moved there; a limited private company was formed and named the 'Keyes Daren Mills Ltd' until 1929, when the firm was called Daren Ltd. S. K. Keyes was also a local Councillor and author of *Dartford Historical Notes*

138 The Grand Hall by the sea, Marine Parade, Margate, *c.* 1885. Here 'Lord' George Sangers opened in 1874 his entertainment centre, which included Italian and Zoological Gardens, Roller Skating, a Ball Room, a Concert Hall and a Restaurant. In 1905 all the animals were sold and the area became an Amusement Park. Sanger was owner of the largest English Circus of the time

139 The 'Old Stagers' are the oldest known Amateur Dramatic Society in the world. They were founded in 1842 and remain an all-male Society, only performing in Canterbury during the Canterbury Cricket Week. Professional and amateur actresses are invited to take part in the productions. The performance of *My Friend the Prince* took place *c.* 1910. On the extreme right is Nigel Playfair

140 The orchestra of the Dartford Young Men's Bible Class, 1905, assisted by a few young ladies

141 The Photographers Club of Tunbridge Wells, 30 May 1891. From left to right: Messrs Spradly, E. R. Ashton, Brampton, W. H. Booty, W. Morgan and Alderman Penn

MILITARY KENT

142   Cadets at the Royal Military Academy, Woolwich, 1864. The Academy existed from 1806 to 1939, when it was transferred and amalgamated with that at Sandhurst

143 'Where is the battle?' Major-General Sir Richard Dacres and his staff at Dartford in 1863. Left to right: Major Reilly, Sir Richard Dacres, Major Milward, Captain Nangle. Sir Richard Dacres was Commandant of the Royal Military Academy, Woolwich 1859–65 and was made General in 1868. Major W. E. M. Reilly was aide-de-camp to Sir Richard Dacres 1856–1859 and was an unrivalled practical artillery man. Major T. W. Milward became Superintendent of the Royal Laboratory 1870–74 and invented light steel guns for mountain service

144 A combined Royal Artillery/Royal Engineers Training Exercise, *c.* 1868. A timber suspension bridge, for swift assault action only, is being constructed across St Mary's Creek, Chatham, and the Artillery are 'testing' it by moving a field gun across it. The bridge leads to St Mary's Island and Gillingham can be seen beyond. This area is now a part of Chatham Dockyard

145 Another combined Royal Artillery/Royal Engineers Training Exercise taking place on St Mary's Island, Chatham, 1868. The Engineers have breached a 'wall' of Gillingham Fort so that the Artillery can take a field gun through it. In the background is the River Medway, with Upnor on the far shore. In 1866 land was bought at Wouldham for a Summer Bridging Camp and, shortly after this photograph was taken, the exercises took place there for six weeks each summer for almost a hundred years

146 A drummer and bugler of the Royal Artillery at Woolwich, 1856. The very young bugler holds a standard bearing the Russian Imperial Eagle, no doubt a trophy from the Crimean War, just ended. His youth would have been no barrier to active service

147 Officers of 'B' Battery, 4th Brigade, the Royal Military Academy, Woolwich in March 1869. Prince Arthur is seated on top of the field gun and Lieut. A. Picard, his aide-de-camp, is standing on his left with his elbow resting on it – he won the V.C. in New Zealand at the assault on Rangiriri in 1873

148 The Band leading a Parade from the Main Gate of the Royal Marine Barracks at Chatham, *c.* 1900. The men are wearing the 'Wolseley' helmet, designed by Sir Garnet Wolseley. The Barracks were pulled down by October 1959

149 Charles Darwin in later life, *c*. 1869. After the voyage of *The Beagle*, he was in poor health and settled at Downe House, near Bromley, from 1842 until his death in 1882. It was a happy home. Darwin was content there with his family, gardens and animals and occupied himself with botanical observations and the publication of his books. Downe House was a school from 1907–1922; it is now the property of the Royal College of Surgeons and is open to the public

150 Charles Dickens' study at Gads Hill Place, near Rochester. Dickens had admired the house during childhood when his family lived in Chatham (1817–1822) and, when it was for sale in his years of success, made it his permanent home from 1860 until his death in 1870. The house is now occupied by a school

151 Charles Dickens, a photograph taken in 1859 when he was 47. In this year he published *A Tale of Two Cities* and decided to make Gads Hill Place his permanent home

152 A group in the porch at Gads Hill Place about one year before Charles Dickens died in 1870 of a cerebral haemorrhage whilst writing *The Mystery of Edwin Drood*

153 Henry Checkley, the last Beadle and Town Crier of Bromley, was a native of the town and carried on his trade as bootmaker for some years. When the office of Beadle was abolished, *c.* 1880, he left the town

154 The Dartford Town Beadle, *c.* 1886, also sold newspapers and posted bills. He was Frederick Batt of 101 Lowfield Street, Dartford, and was probably the son of Thomas Batt, his predecessor, who proclaimed the Accession of William IV in 1830

155 'Count Antonio' or 'Old Tony', a Street Trader, walking past William Berry's Grocery Store at No. 68 Queen Street, Rochester, *c.* 1910

156 Mr Joseph Sparrowhawk of Edenbridge photographed in 1872. Before the S.E. Railway came, as a young man he walked the 29 miles to London and back three times weekly carrying a consignment of boots on his back and returning with leather: Edenbridge had a noted boot trade in the nineteenth century. Joseph walked to London and back in one day for the Coronation of Queen Victoria in 1837 and was the first to carry the news of the peace to Buckhurst at the end of the Crimean War in 1856. When Edenbridge Station opened in 1842, he became Parcel Porter and Carrier from Edenbridge and Westerham, walking 12 miles per day for the next 50 years. Mr Sparrowhawk died in 1898 aged 86

157 The Revd James Edward Newell, M.A., in clerical walking-out dress. He was Vicar of St Peter and St Paul, the Parish Church of Bromley, from 1826–1865

FLYING

HON. C.S.ROLLS'S
CONQUEST OF THE CHANNEL,
2ND June, 1910.
RETURN JOURNEY DONE
WITHOUT LANDING.

Start from Dover · · · · 6.30 p.m.
Over Sangatte, France · · 7.15 p.m.
Return to Dover · · · · 8.0 p.m.

158 The Hon. C. S. Roll's non-stop return flight over the English Channel took place on 2 June 1910 in a Short-built Wright bi-plane. He flew from the grounds of a Dover School to Sangatter, where he dropped greetings to the Aero Club de France. The 80-mile return flight took 90 minutes, and Rolls circled Dover Castle before landing in a field. One month later he was killed in a flying accident. His memorial may be seen on the Marine Parade, Dover

159 Five Oak Green, near Tonbridge, 1911. The plane resembles a Bristol Box-kite of this date and was of great interest in these early days of aviation

160 The 'Colonel Balloon' being prepared for Colonel Frederick Brine, R.E. to make his attempt to cross the channel from Canterbury on 4 March 1882. It was unsuccessful, but he did travel from Hythe to Hervelingham on 15 August 1884, for which he received the Gold Medal of the Balloon Society. He died in 1890. Colonel Brine is standing in front of the balloon

161 M. and Mme Louis Blériot received by the Mayor and civic dignitaries of Dover on the steps of The Lord Warden Hotel on 26 July 1909, after Blériot had flown from Les Baraques, in France, to Dover in a Blériot XI Monoplane. The Blériot Cross, representing the shape of an aircraft, marks the spot on the cliff where he landed. The Lord Warden Hotel is now the stores and offices of British Rail

FIRE-FIGHTING

162 Rearing horses at the National Fire Brigade's Union demonstrations held in the Castle Grounds during Tonbridge Week 1909. The Tonbridge Town Fire Brigade was inaugurated in May 1901 and the Fire Station built on a portion of the Castle Grounds; previously fire fighters had been under the surveyance of the members of the Local Board

163 A fire engine made especially for Country Houses and powered by the Daimler Petroleum Engine. This model was exhibited by the Hon. Evelyn Ellis at the Exhibition of Horseless Vehicles at Tunbridge Wells in October 1895. The group of firemen belonged to the Tunbridge Wells Volunteer Fire Brigade and the Hon. Evelyn Ellis stands on the right of the engine

164 Members of three Fire Brigades and Cathedral Staff had just quenched a fire in the roof of Canterbury Cathedral when this photograph was taken. The fire broke out at 1.00 p.m. on Tuesday 3 September 1872. The Phoenix Brigade was a private fire-fighting organisation belonging to the Phoenix Insurance Company

THE END OF THE AGE

165   The German Emperor, Kaiser Wilhelm II, arrives by special train at 4.50 p.m. on 23 May 1910 at Port Victoria, Isle of Grain. He had been to the funeral of his Uncle, King Edward VII. The Emperor was greeted by a Royal Salute from a Guard of Honour of 100 men from the D.C.L.I. commanded by Captain Olivier. Three rousing 'Hochs' came from the crew of the German Imperial Yacht *Hohenzollern* which waited to convey him to Flushing next morning, when warships in Sheerness Harbour dressed ship and fired 21 gun salutes as he passed. The Emperor is followed by General Barker and Captain Olivier. The Station at Port Victoria was opened on 2 September 1882 and was used by Queen Victoria and her relations when making family visits

166 The Civic Dignitaries of Tenterden in procession on the occasion of the Proclamation of King George V on 9 May 1910

167 A skipping race for girls during the festivities in Tonbridge High Street to celebrate the Coronation of King George V and Queen Mary on 22 June 1911

168 King Edward VII's Birthday Parade proceeding along the Marine Parade, Dover, *c.* 1905. One horse and rider are causing confusion in the ranks opposite the Saluting Base. The Sovereign's Official Birthday had not been instituted so this must have been held on 9 October – an Indian Summer judging by the open parasols and light dresses of the ladies